THE MIRACLES
OF
JESUS

THE MIRACLES
OF
JESUS

retold from the Bible and illustrated by

TOMIE dePAOLA

The Lutterworth Press
Cambridge

The Lutterworth Press
P.O. Box 60
Cambridge
CB1 2NT

British Library Cataloguing-in-Publication Data:
A catalogue record for this book is
available from the British Library.

Printed in Italy

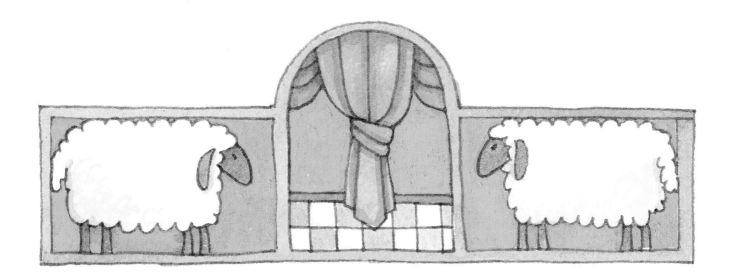

The miracles in this book were adapted from the following
New Testament chapters and verses:

After Jesus of Nazareth was baptized, he began his public life,
and he performed many miracles.

The Wedding at Cana

There was a wedding at Cana in Galilee, and the mother of Jesus was there.

Jesus and his disciples were also invited.

The wine for the wedding ran out, and Jesus' mother said to him, "They have no wine."

Jesus answered, "Mother, why do you turn to me? My hour has not yet come."

Then his mother went to the servants and said, "Do whatever he tells you."

Standing near were six stone jars, used to hold water for the Jewish rites of purification. Each jar held twenty to thirty gallons.

Jesus said to the servants, "Fill each jar with water," and they did as they were told.

Then Jesus said, "Now draw some out and take it to the steward," which the servants did.

The steward tasted the water now turned into wine. He did not know where it came from, but the servants who had drawn the water did.

The steward called the bridegroom to him and said, "Most people serve the best wine first and save the cheaper wine until everyone has had plenty to drink. But you have kept the best wine until last."

Thus, at Cana in Galilee, did Jesus begin his miracles. And his disciples believed in him.

The Catch of Fishes

As Jesus was standing and preaching by the lake of Gennesaret, the people crowded around him to hear the word of God.

Jesus noticed two boats close to the edge of the water, for the fishermen had come ashore and were washing their nets.

Jesus got into one of the boats, which belonged to Simon, and asked him to row out a little from the shore. Then Jesus continued his teaching from his seat on the boat.

When he had finished speaking, Jesus said to Simon, "Put out into deep water and let down the nets for a catch."

"Master," Simon replied, "we worked hard all night long and caught nothing, but if you say so, I will let the nets down."

Simon and his men did this and before they knew it, they had caught so many fish that the nets began to break.

They called to their partners and soon both boats were so full that they were in danger of sinking.

When Simon saw this, he fell at Jesus' knees and cried, "Leave me, Lord, for I am a sinner."

And Simon and all his companions, including his partners James and John, the sons of Zebedee, were astonished by the huge catch of fish they had made.

Then Jesus said, "Simon, do not be afraid. From now on you shall be catching men."

And they brought their boats back to land, left everything, and followed Jesus.

The Calming of the Storm

One day, Jesus got into a boat with his disciples and said, "Let us cross over to the other side of the lake."

So they set sail and as the boat moved along, Jesus fell asleep. A sudden storm came up and water began to pour into the boat, so that they were in great danger.

The disciples went to Jesus and woke him, saying, "Master, master, we are sinking."

Jesus arose and rebuked the raging wind and stormy waters. Suddenly the wind stopped and the waves ceased and all was calm again.

Then Jesus said to his disciples, "Where is your faith?" The disciples were afraid and said one to another, "Who can this be? He gives orders to the wind and the waves, and they obey him."

The Loaves and the Fishes

When Jesus withdrew to the far shore of the Sea of Galilee, a large crowd of people followed him, for they had seen the signs he gave in healing the sick.

Jesus then went up to the hillside and sat down with his disciples.

This was near the time of the great Jewish festival of Passover.

Jesus looked up and saw the large crowds coming up to him, so he said to his disciple Philip, "Where can we buy bread for all these people?"

Jesus only said this to test Philip, for he knew what he was going to do.

Philip answered, "Two hundred denarii would not buy enough to give everyone a small piece."

The disciple Andrew said, "There is a boy here who has five barley loaves and two fishes, but what good will that do with such a great number of people to feed?"

Jesus said, "Make the people sit down." There was plenty of grass, and as many as five thousand people sat.

Then Jesus took the loaves, blessed them, and gave them to all who were there. He did the same with the two fish.

When all had eaten their fill, Jesus said to his disciples, "Collect the pieces left over, so that nothing may be wasted."

This the disciples did, and they filled twelve baskets with the leftovers from the meal of five barley loaves and two fishes.

The people witnessing the sign said, "This really must be the prophet who is come into the world."

And seeing that the people were about to come and make him king, Jesus fled and withdrew to the hills by himself.

Jesus Walks on the Water

Before Jesus went up to the hills to pray, he told his disciples to get into their boat and go ahead of him to the other side of the lake.

In the early morning, before dawn, the boat was a good distance from shore and was being tossed about by the rough waters.

Suddenly, the disciples saw Jesus walking toward them over the lake. They were so frightened that they called out in terror, "It is a ghost!"

But Jesus spoke to them, saying, "Take heart, it is I. Don't be afraid!"

Then Simon, who was also called Peter, cried out to Jesus. "Lord," he said, "if it is you, tell me to come to you over the water."

"Come," said Jesus. So Simon Peter got out of the boat and he too began to walk on the water.

But the wind was blowing so hard that Simon Peter grew frightened and began to sink. "Lord, save me," he cried.

Jesus reached out his hand at once and caught hold of him. "Oh, man of little faith," Jesus said, "why did you doubt?"

Then, as Jesus helped Simon Peter into the boat, the wind stopped and the other disciples fell on their knees and said, "Truly, you are the Son of God."

The Paralyzed Man

On one of the days that Jesus was teaching, Pharisees and teachers of the law were listening. People had come from every village of Galilee and from Judea and Jerusalem. And the power of the Lord to heal was with Jesus.

Then some men appeared, carrying a paralyzed man on a bed, but they could not get in to where Jesus was because of the crowd.

So, they went up to the roof, and, removing some of the tiles, lowered the man on his bed into the gathering around Jesus.

And when he saw their faith, Jesus said, "My friend, your sins are forgiven."

Now, the lawyers and the Pharisees began to say to themselves, "Who is this man who says such blasphemous things? Only God alone can forgive sins."

But Jesus knew what they were thinking and said, "Why do you think such thoughts? What is easier to say, 'Your sins are forgiven,' or 'Stand up and walk'?

"But I will prove to you that the Son of Man has the right on earth to forgive sins." He turned to the paralyzed man and said, "I say to you, rise, take up your bed and walk."

And before everyone's eyes, the man rose to his feet, picked up his bed and went home, praising God.

Everyone there was amazed and praised God, too. Filled with awe, they said, "We have seen strange things today."

The Cure of the Man at
the Pool of Bethesda

At the time of one of the Jewish festivals, Jesus went up to Jerusalem.

There by the sheep gate is a pool which in Hebrew is called Bethesda, because it has five porches.

In these porches lay many sick, paralyzed, blind and lame people. They were waiting for the water in the pool to move, for from time to time an angel came down and stirred it up. The first person to enter the water after this disturbance was cured of whatever ailment he suffered from.

Among these people was a man who had been crippled for thirty-eight years. When Jesus saw him and knew that he had been ill a long time, he asked, "Do you want to be well again?"

"Sir," replied the sick man, "I have no one to help me get into the water when it is disturbed. And while I am on my way to the water, someone always gets there before me."

Jesus answered, "Rise, take up your sleeping mat and walk."

The man was healed at once, and he picked up his mat and walked away.

The Centurion's Servant

There was in Capernaum a centurion who had a highly favored servant. This servant was ill and near death.

Having heard about Jesus, the centurion asked some Jewish elders to go to Jesus and ask him to come and heal the centurion's servant.

The elders went to Jesus and said, "This centurion is worthy of this favor from you. He is a friend of the Jewish nation, and it was he who built our synagogue."

So Jesus went with the elders, but when he was not very far from the house, the centurion sent friends to Jesus, with this message: "Lord, do not trouble yourself, for I am not worthy to have you come under my roof.

"And that is why I did not presume to come to you in person. But only say the word, and my servant will be healed.

"For in my position I myself am a man under orders and have soldiers under me. I say to one 'Go,' and he goes; and to another 'Come,' and he comes; and to my servant, 'Do this,' and he does it."

When Jesus heard this, he admired the centurion, and he turned to the people that followed him and said, "I tell you, not even in Israel have I found faith like this."

And when the centurion's friends returned to the house, they found the servant in perfect health.

Jesus Opens the Eyes of
the Blind Man

One time, when Jesus was approaching Jericho, there was a blind man sitting by the side of the road, begging.

Hearing the crowd, he asked what was happening, and he was told that Jesus of Nazareth was passing by.

So the blind man called out, "Jesus, son of David, have pity on me."

The people in front scolded him and told him to be quiet. But, he cried out all the more, "Jesus, son of David, have pity on me."

Jesus stopped and had the blind man brought to him.

Jesus asked him, "What do you want me to do for you?" The blind man answered, "Lord, let me see again."

Then Jesus said to him, "Receive your sight. Your faith has made you well."

Instantly, the man's sight returned, and he followed Jesus, praising God. And all the people who saw it praised God as well.

Jesus Heals the Lepers

On the way to Jerusalem, Jesus passed along the border between Samaria and Galilee.

As he entered a village, ten lepers came out to meet him.

They stood some way off and cried to Jesus, "Master, have mercy on us."

When Jesus saw them, he said, "Go and show yourselves to the priests." And as they went, they found themselves cleansed.

Then one of them, seeing himself healed, turned back, praising God with a loud voice.

He threw himself at Jesus' feet and thanked him. Now, the man was a Samaritan.

At this, Jesus said, "Were not all ten made clean? Where are the other nine?

"Could no one be found to return and give praise to God except this foreigner?"

Then Jesus said to the man, "Rise and go your way. Your faith has cured you."

The Daughter of Jairus

When Jesus was speaking, an official of the synagogue named Jairus came to him. He begged Jesus to return with him to his house, for his only daughter, who was about twelve years of age, was dying.

As Jesus went, crowds of people pressed against him. A woman who had suffered from a flow of blood for twelve years came up behind him and touched the hem of his garment. Immediately, the flow of blood ceased.

Jesus said, "Who touched me?" When everyone denied it, the disciples said, "Master, it is the crowd pressing against you."

But Jesus said, "Somebody touched me. I felt that power had gone out from me."

Seeing herself discovered, the woman came forward, trembling, and fell at Jesus' feet. Before all the people, she declared why she had touched Jesus and how she had been immediately healed.

And Jesus said to her, "Daughter, your faith has made you well. Go in peace."

While he was still speaking, a man from Jairus's house came and said, "Your daughter is dead. Do not trouble the master any further."

But when he heard this Jesus said, "Do not be afraid, only have faith and she shall be well."

And when they came to the house, Jesus allowed no one to go in with him except Peter and John and James and the child's father and mother.

All were weeping and mourning for her. But Jesus said, "Do not weep. She is not dead. She is asleep."

And the people only laughed at him, knowing that she was dead.

Jesus took her by the hand and said, "Child, arise."

And her spirit returned and she got up at once. Then Jesus told them to give her something to eat.

Her parents were amazed but Jesus ordered them not to tell anyone what had happened.

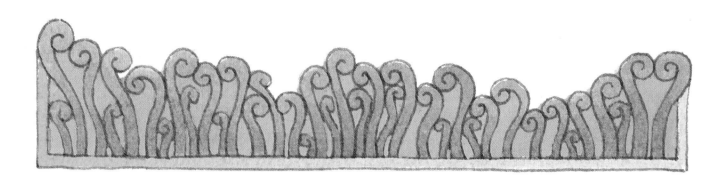

The Raising of Lazarus

When Lazarus, the brother of Mary and Martha, died, Jesus came to them.

Martha went out to meet him while Mary sat in the house.

Martha said to Jesus, "If you had been here, my brother would not have died, but I know that, even now, whatever you ask of God, he will grant you."

"Your brother," said Jesus, "will rise again."

"I know he will rise again," said Martha, "at the resurrection on the last day."

Then Jesus said, "I am the resurrection and the life. If anyone believes in me, even though he dies, he will live. And whoever lives and believes in me will never die. Do you believe this?"

"Yes, Lord," she said. "I believe that you are the Christ, the Son of God, who was to come into the world."

When she had said this, Martha went and called her sister Mary. "The master is here," she said, "and wants to see you."

Jesus had not yet come into the village, but was still at the place where he met Martha.

So, Mary rose up quickly and went to him.

The Jews who were in the house, mourning Lazarus's death, saw Mary rush out, and, thinking that she was going to the tomb to weep, followed her.

Mary went to where Jesus was, and she fell at his feet, weeping. "Lord," she said, "if you had been here, my brother would not have died."

When Jesus saw her weeping and the Jews who had followed her weeping also, he said in great distress, with a sigh that came straight from his heart, "Where have you laid him?"

The people said, "Come and see, Lord."

Jesus wept.

So the Jews said, "See how he loved Lazarus." But others said, "Could not this man who has opened the eyes of the blind have done something to keep Lazarus from dying?"

When Jesus reached the tomb, which was a cave with a stone to close the opening, he said, "Take the stone away!"

"But Lord," said Martha, "by now he will smell. This is the fourth day."

Jesus answered, "Have I not told you that if you believe you will see the glory of God?"

So they took away the stone. Jesus lifted up his eyes and said, "Father, I thank you for hearing my prayer."

Then he raised his voice and called out, "Lazarus, come forth."

The dead man came out, his hands and feet bound in linen bands, his face wrapped in cloth. And Jesus said, "Unbind him and let him go."